AMERICAN COMBAT JUDO

AMERICAN Combat JUDO

by BERNARD J. COSNECK

200 PHOTOGRAPHS
ILLUSTRATING JIU JITSU
WRESTLING, FOOT-FIGHTING
AND POLICE TACTICS

Also by Bernard J. Cosneck:

How to Fight Tough (with Lt. Jack Dempsey)

American Combat Judo
186 Photographs, Illustrating Jiu-Jitsu, Police Tactics, French Foot Fighting, and Wrestling
by Bernard J. Cosneck

Original edition published 1959 by Bernard J. Cosneck
Reprint edition published 2006 by Paladin Press

ISBN 13: 978-1-58160-531-0
Printed in the United States of America

Published by Paladin Press, a division of
Paladin Enterprises, Inc.
Gunbarrel Tech Center
7077 Winchester Circle
Boulder, Colorado 80301 USA, +1.303.443.7250

Direct inquiries and/or orders to the above address.

Visit our website at www.paladin-press.com

PREFACE

This handbook of American Judo is a thorough study in the methods and techniques of hand-fighting. It is based upon the classic jiu-jutsu but incorporates the most recent improvements in the scientific development of modes of personal combat. It also borrows from wrestling, boxing and la Savatte (footfighting), those special features that are peculiarly adapted for a system of hand-fighting.

The purpose of The American Judo is twofold. The first is to develop a technique of disabling and, if necessary, seriously injuring an opponent. The second and of no lesser importance is to give the reader adequate skill and knowledge in defending himself against an assailant. In both instances it is perfectly obvious how important it is to perfect to the highest degree the mechanical efficiency of the various holds, grips, etc., that are employed in the system of American Judo. It cannot be over-emphasized that the slightest defection in the application of any given hold may mean serious injury. Furthermore, every superfluous movement, no matter how slight, must be eliminated. The essence of success in the method of American Judo is speed, combined with a complete knowledge of the proper moves based on the element of surprise. Another point is that the holds taught are broken with the greatest difficulty. Each hold is created with one dominant purpose: to secure the maximum effect with the greatest economy of time, movement and effort.

The large number and variety of holds and maneuvers have been presented not with the intention of having the student master each and every one; rather, they have been enumerated and illustrated to afford him an opportunity to select those best fitted to his personal physical equipment. The hold that one man excels in cannot always be mastered by another. In this connection it is well to remember that absolute proficiency in a few holds is a wiser policy than an incomplete mastery of a hundred.

SUGGESTIONS TO THE READER

1. Every move must be made with a snap or jerk. A slow move is absolutely worthless.
2. Any of the holds in this book can result in extreme injury, therefore, exercise extreme caution in practice.
3. Don't try to resist your opponent, on the contrary, give way to his pressure and use his original force and momentum to his own disadvantage. In fact, the counter move for most Judo holds is to move with your opponent's hold faster than he expects you to. In that way you can often escape from an otherwise unbreakable hold.
4. The secret of falling is to be completely relaxed. This is often quite difficult, because when a person feels himself falling his instinctive reaction is to tense his muscles. Although instinctive, this reaction is to be avoided because muscular tension places a strain on the bones to which the muscles are attached, enabling these bones to be more easily injured.
5. Work all the holds from both sides so as not to limit yourself to becoming "one-sided" in your abilities.
6. Every move in Judo should be made with a maximum of speed and carried through to its logical conclusion. Be sure that you have the procedures clearly in mind. Never stop a movement half way because injuries to yourself might easily result.
7. All moves should be smooth and flow one into the other with no awkward halts or delays between them.

CONTENTS

	Page
PREFACE	V
SUGGESTIONS TO THE READER	VII
DISABLING BLOWS	11
Hack and Jab	12
Chart of Disabling Blows	13
HOLDS AND LOCKS	21
Rear Arm Strangle	22
Grab Belt or Crotch	24
Wrist Hold Variations	26
Grab from Behind—Arms Free	28
Grab from Behind—Arms Locked	30
Arm Drag from Behind	32
BREAKS AND RELEASES	35
Break from Front Body Scissors	36
Break from Rear Body Scissors	38
Break from Full Nelson	40
Break from Hammer Lock	42
Break from Front Finger Strangle	44
Break from Grab Belt and Elbow	46
Break from Rear Strangle	48
Break from Arm Strangle	50
Break from Hand Clasp	52
Break from Front Bear Hug	54
THROWS AND TRIPS	57
Shoulder Twist into Strangle	58
Hip Throw	60
Shoulder Throw	62
Tip Over	64
Counter for Chest Push	66
Pile Driver	68
Ankle or Cuff Jerk	70
Lapel Throw	72
Trip from Rear	74
Trip from Behind	76
POLICE TACTICS	79
Fighting Two Men at Once	80
Rope Strangle	82
Hammer Lock Come-Along	84
Removing an Unwilling Person from a Chair	86
Disarming an Assailant Who Has a Pistol Pointed at Your Back	88
Disarming an Assailant Who Is Facing You with a Pistol	92
Disarming Opponent of Club	94
Crossed Arm Come-Along	96
Resuscitation	98

POLICE TACTICS—(Continued)

Taking an Unwilling Prisoner 100
How to Search a Prisoner 102
Blocking Hip or Shoulder Throw 104
Disarming Opponent of a Knife 106
Blocking Kick to Testicles 108
Arm Hack Come-Along 110
Arm Twist 112
Wrist Lock Come-Along 114
Attack from the Ground 116

SITUATIONS 119
Being Attacked from the Rear 121
Being Strangled with Hands 121
Being Strangled with Forearm 121
Being Grasped by the Wrists 121
Being Attacked While Lying Face Down 121
Being Rushed Head-On 122
Fighting Face to Face 122
Making an Attack from the Rear 122

DISABLING BLOWS

THE HACK AND THE JAB IN JUDO

The hack is a hand blow delivered with the little finger side of the open hand. The fingers are held extended, stiff and close together. The thumb may or may not be extended. The blow is given with a swift, sharp, hacking movement with such abrupt force that it can either break a bone or paralyze a nerve. Continual practice of pounding the underside of the hand upon a hard, flat object such as a table is advised for toughening the striking surface of the hand. After the hand is thus prepared it can be further toughened by pounding the edge or corner of an object.

When administering the blow, contact is made with that surface of the edge of the hand between the wrist and the base of the little finger. The fingers themselves are not used in striking, because they may slide over each other and make the blow less effective.

The jab is made with the closed fist, the knuckle of the middle finger protruding. The blow with the fist covers too great an area, whereas the knuckle of the finger, being pointed, will localize the blow and thereby intensify it.

CHART OF DISABLING BLOWS

Type of Blow	Areas Affected	Reactions
Fig. 3. Hack	Upper Lip	pain, broken nose, loosened teeth
Fig. 4. Hack	Temple and ears	headache, pain, possible unconsciousness
Fig. 5. Hack	Wrist or bones of thumb	possible fracture
Fig. 6. Hack	Biceps muscles	temporary paralysis of arm
Fig. 7. Hack, punch, squeeze or knee		unbearable agony, complete paralysis, collapse
Fig. 8. Hack	Adam's Apple	physical collapse, gagging and nausea
Fig. 9. Hack or fist blow	kidneys	temporary paralysis, physical collapse
Fig. 10. Hack or jab	collar bone	fracture
Fig. 11. Hack	sides of jaw	possible dislocation and unconsciousness
Fig. 12. Hack or jab	temple bones	unconsciousness and possible bone fracture
Fig. 13. Hack	bridge of nose	fracture
Fig. 14. Hack (Rabbit punch)	back of neck	stunning pain, possible unconsciousness, followed by severe headache

CHART OF DISABLING BLOWS

Continued

Type of Blow	Areas Affected	Reactions
Fig. 15. Thumb jab	throat below Adam's Apple	gagging, nausea
Fig. 16. Thumb jab	tissue over eyes	pain
Fig. 17. Thumb jab	hollow of armpit	pain
Fig. 18. Thumb jab	behind ear lobe	pain, temporary disability
Fig. 19. Thumb jab	tissue between jawbone and throat	pain
Fig. 20. Thumb jab	calf	internal pain
Fig. 21. Knuckle dig	sides of spine	excruciating pain
Fig. 22. Punch	pectoral or arm pit	pain, disabling arm
Fig. 23. Punch and twist of fist at point of contact	solar plexus	nausea, physical collapse
Fig. 24. Clap of hands over ears	ears	rupture and pain
Fig. 25. Stamp heel	instep	fracture and pain
Fig. 26. Clawed hand	nostrils	torn and lacterated tissues, extreme pain.

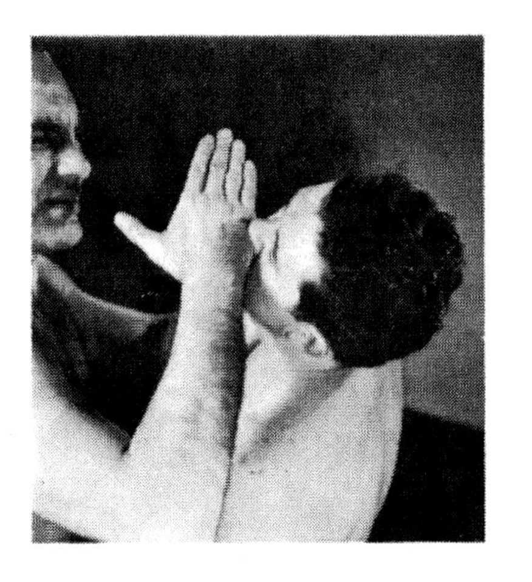

Fig. 3

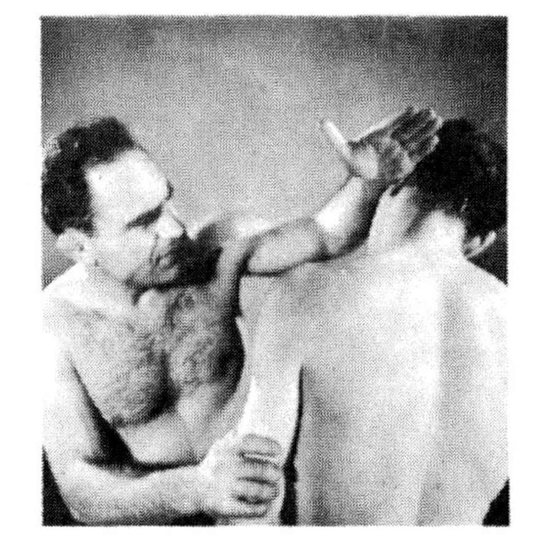

Fig. 4

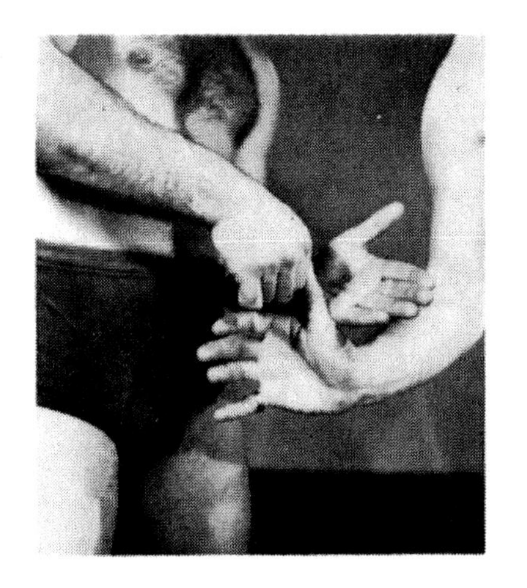

Fig. 5

Fig. 6

Fig. 7

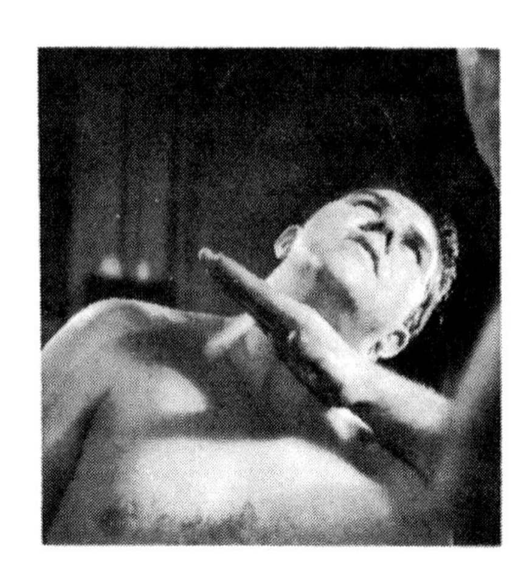

Fig. 8

Fig. 9

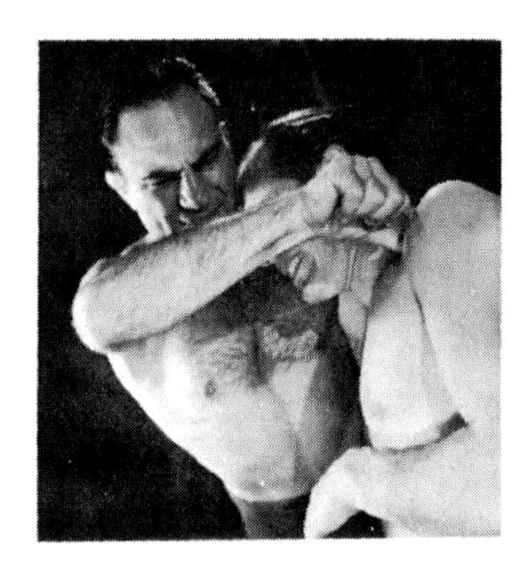

Fig. 10

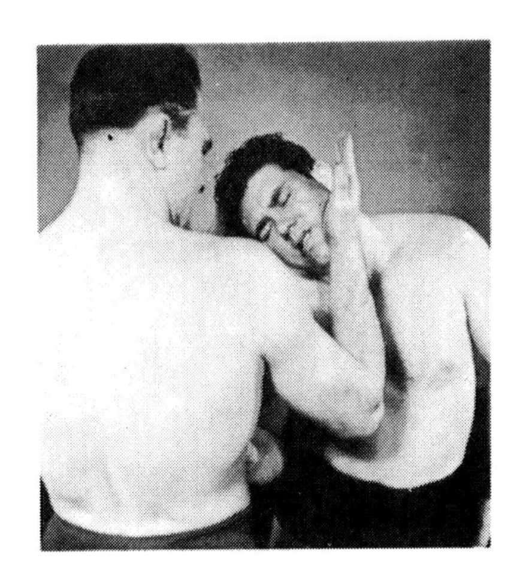

Fig. 11

Fig. 12

Fig. 13

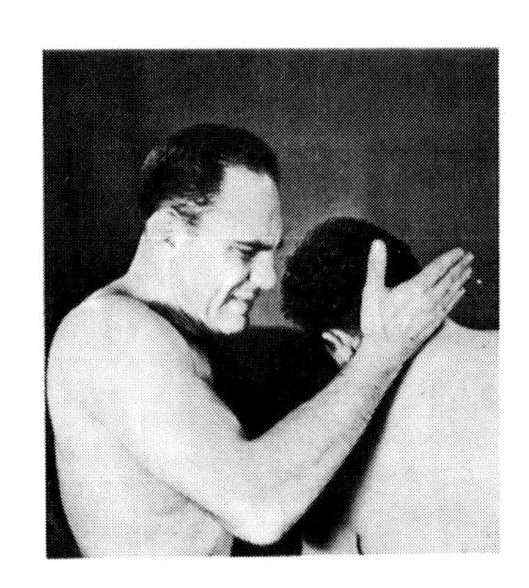

Fig. 14

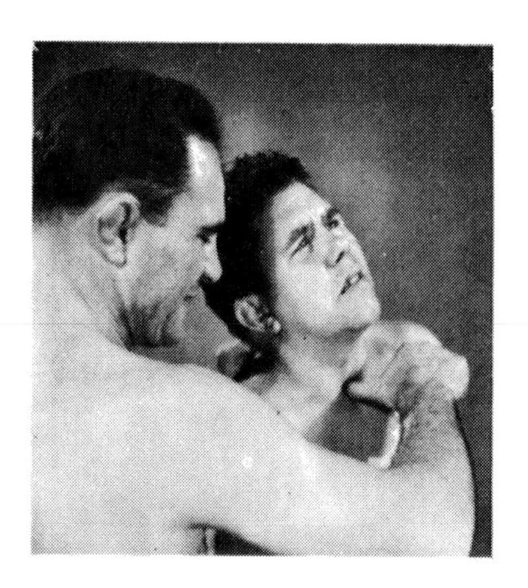

Fig. 15

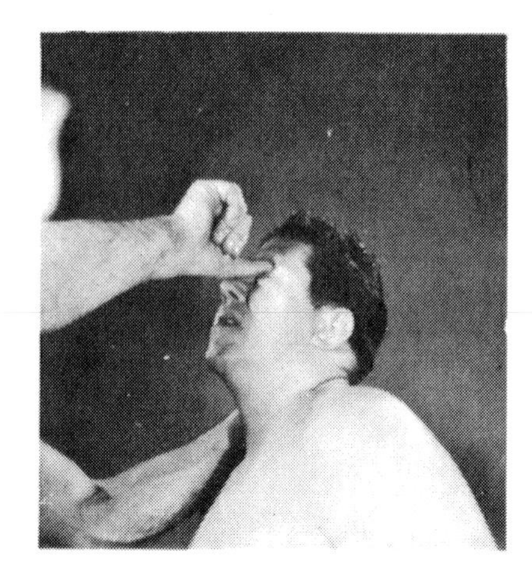

Fig. 16

Fig. 17

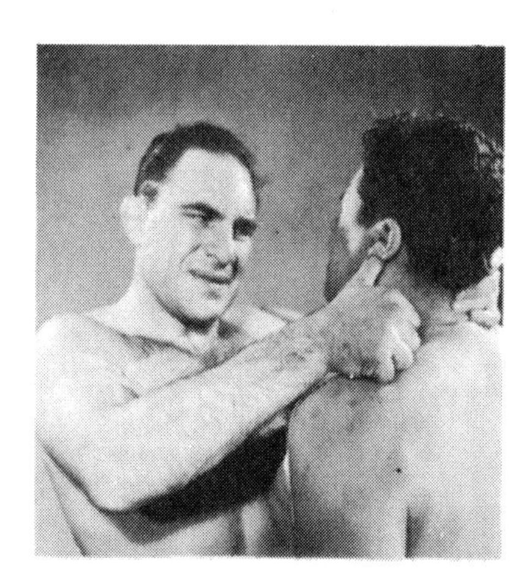

Fig. 18

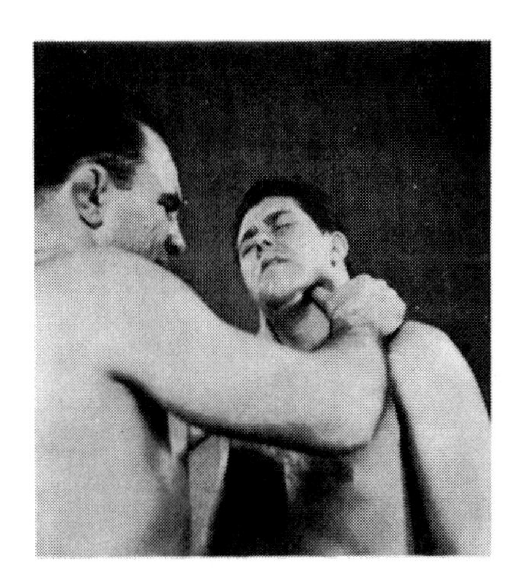

Fig. 19

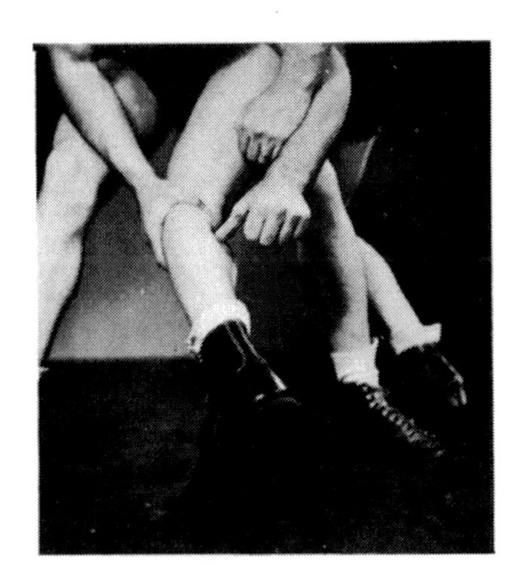

Fig. 20

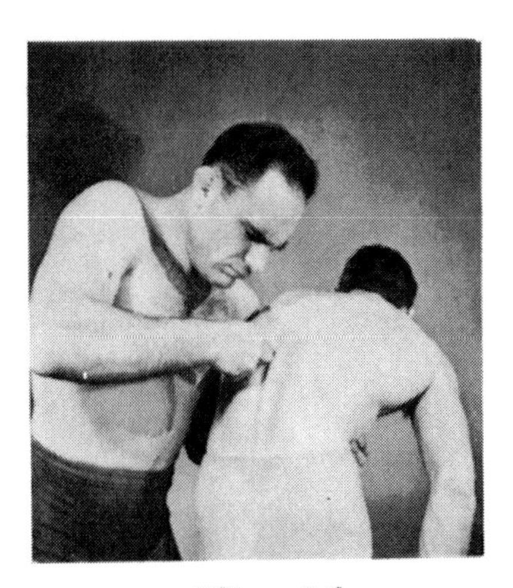

Fig. 21

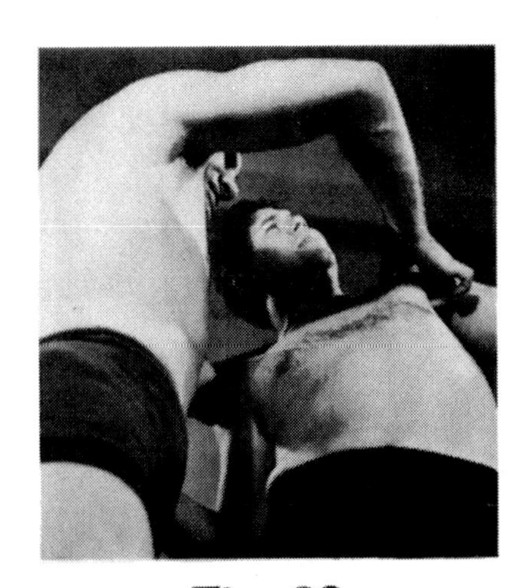

Fig. 22

Fig. 23

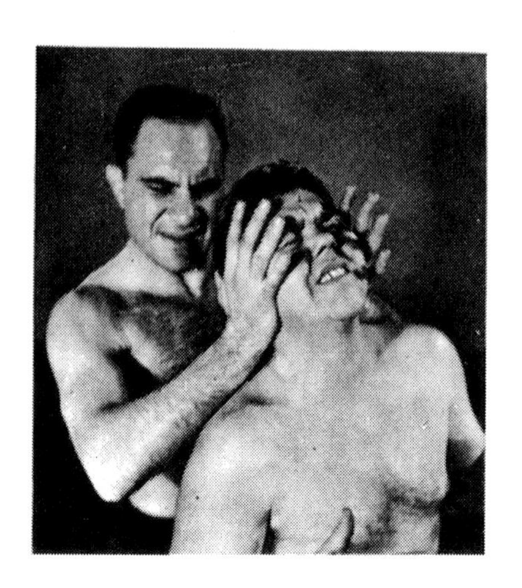

Fig. 24

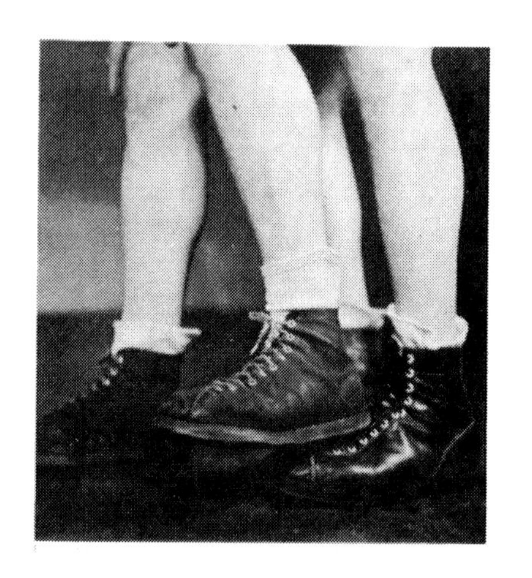

Fig. 25

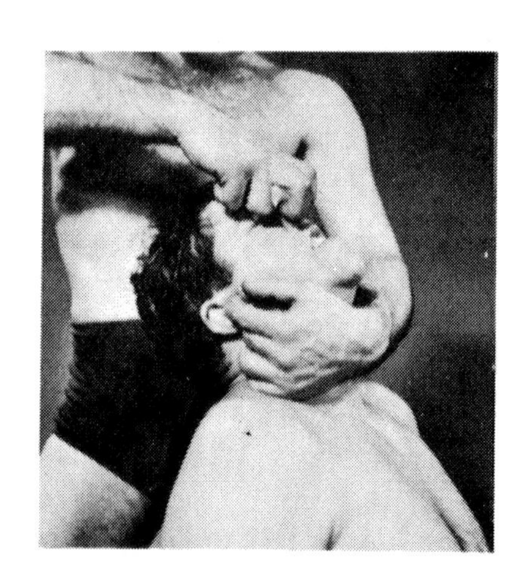

Fig. 26

HOLDS AND LOCKS

REAR ARM STRANGLE

In executing an arm strangle, your arm must be in direct contact with your opponent's throat. The hold is worthless if his chin prevents contact with his throat. It is essential to exert the maximum pressure immediately rather than gradually because your opponent might squirm himself into a less dangerous position.

POSITION: You are standing behind your opponent.

ACTION:

1. Place your left arm around opponent s neck with your wrist bone pressing into his Adam's apple (Fig. 27).
2. Then place the back of your right arm (above the elbow) across his right shoulder and clasp your right biceps with your left hand (Fig. 28).
3. Bend your right arm toward your left hand and place it behind his neck and grasp your left shoulder or biceps with your right hand (Fig. 29).
4. Pull backwards with your left arm and push forward with your right in a scissors-like motion, thus strangling him (Fig. 30).

NOTE: If opponent is taller than you and the hold is awkward or difficult to perform after you have encircled his throat with your left arm (or even before), grab his hair with your right hand and pull his head down backwards until he is down to your size. Then continue with the hold.

Fig. 27

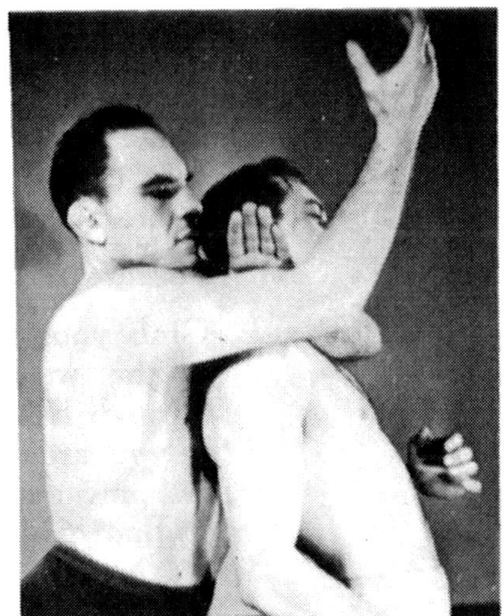

Fig. 28

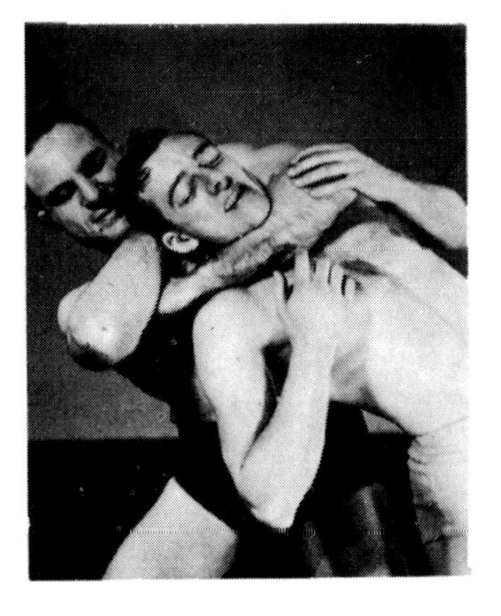

Fig. 29

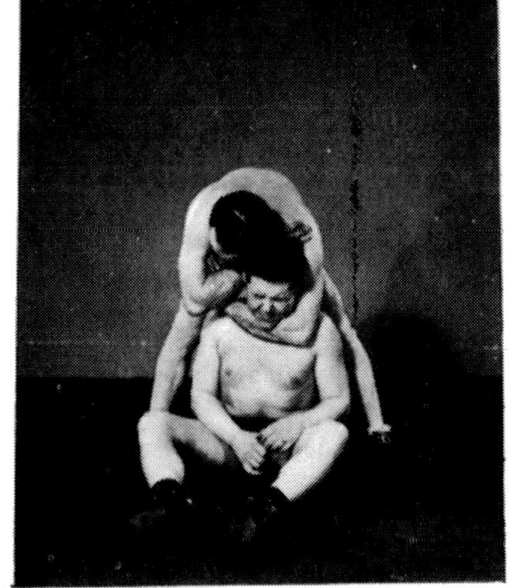

Fig. 30

GRAB BELT OR CROTCH

Very often when you are facing and talking to a belligerent opponent, it is quite obvious that trouble between you is imminent. In that case don't wait for him to take the initiative but go into action yourself.

POSITION: You are facing your opponent.

ACTION:
1: Grab your opponent's belt or his clothes at the waist, or else place your hands through his crotch (Fig. 31).
2. If you are using your right arm for this grasping purpose, pull it sharply backward so that his body is arched forward.
3. At the same time shove your left forearm forcibly against his face or throat, pushing the upper part of his body back (Fig. 32).
4. At the same time place your left foot behind him, then bend your left knee so that his arched body lies backward over your left knee (Fig. 33).
5. Now that you have him stretched helplessly over your thigh, you can hack his throat with your left hand or deliver a blow to his testicles with your right elbow without changing your grip.

Fig. 31

Fig. 32

Fig. 33

WRIST HOLD VARIATIONS

In combat you will frequently grasp your adversary's wrist, bend and twist it. From this position you can proceed to various holds.

POSTION: You have twisted and bent your opponent's wrist.

ACTION:
1. Hack opponent's throat with your free left hand (Fig. 34).
2. Twist wrist to the right and simultaneously jerk his left elbow up with your left. This action should result in tearing ligaments, muscles and tendons of his shoulder.
3. Twist the wrist. Place your left foot outside and behind his left heel and trip him. Your left hand can assist by pushing at his chest or face (Fig. 35).
4. Twist the wrist. Drop to your right knee; place your extended left outside of his left. Trip him.
5. Twist the wrist, step forward on his right foot and bring your left knee into his testicles (Fig. 36).
6. If your opponent has his fist clenched, it will be difficult to twist his wrist. In that event, grasp his fist with your hands, jerk his arm to you abruptly and immediately twist the fist to the right, carrying opponent to the ground on his left side. Do not delay between jerking the arm and twisting the fist (Fig. 37).
7. If you have difficulty in twisting adversary's wrist, hack at his wrist with your left hand. This will immediately sap his arm strength and enable you to apply the twist.

Fig. 34

Fig. 35

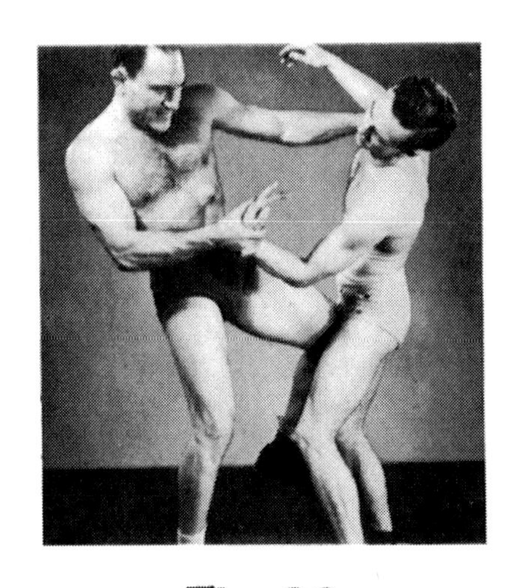

Fig. 36

Fig. 37

GRAB FROM BEHIND—ARMS FREE

Sometimes, when you are grabbed from behind your arms will be free. If you work quickly there will be no difficulty in escaping the hold.

POSITION: Your opponent has your body encircled from the rear, your arms free (Fig. 38).

ACTION:
1. Bend forward, stretch your arms outside your legs and grasp his ankles or trouser cuffs (Fig. 39).
2. Stand up abruptly, dragging his ankles with you. He will be thrown on his back (Fig. 40).
3. Then let the whole weight of your body fall on his stomach and execute any of the toe holds ordinarily used in wrestling.

Fig. 38

Fig. 39

Fig. 40

GRAB FROM BEHIND—ARMS LOCKED

As a rule, an opponent who has had training in combat, particularly a wrestler, will always try to get behind you. This is ordinarily a safe and effective position from which to work. However, the informed combatant can meet the situation and by means of the actions described below gain the upper hand.

POSITION: Your opponent has your arms and body encircled from the rear.

ACTION:
1. Drive the heel of your right foot into the small bones of his right instep. These bones have little resistance and can be broken as easily as an eggshell, or,
2. Put the edge of your right foot against his shin bone just below the knee and scrape your shoe down the entire length of his (Fig. 41), or.
3. Grab his testicles with your hand and squeeze (Fig. 42), or,
4. Snap your head back into his nose (Fig. 43), or,
5. Try to twist your arms free and jab your elbow backward into his face. Or,
6. Shuffle your legs to compel your opponent to move. If he spreads his legs, bend forward and bring your heel backward into his testicles (Fig. 44).

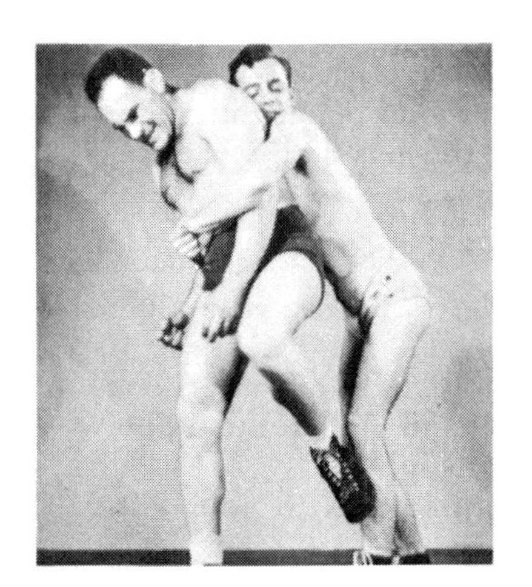

Fig. 41

Fig. 42

Fig. 43

Fig. 44

ARM DRAG FROM BEHIND

It is always desirable to be in back of your opponent. Since this hold will enable you to realize this position, it is therefore of great importance.

POSITION: You are facing your opponent.

ACTION:
1. Grasp opponent's left wrist in your right hand (Fig 45).
2. Step forward on your left foot and hook your free cupped hand under the upper part of his left arm (Fig. 46).
3. Throw his left captured arm to your left. Release it (Fig. 47).
4. Without any hesitation grab his left shoulder with your left hand; pull him around and step behind him.
5. As your opponent is being twisted around, wrap your right hand around his waist to secure your newly acquired position (Fig. 48).

Fig. 45

Fig. 46

Fig. 47

Fig. 48

BREAKS AND RELEASES

BREAK FROM FRONT BODY SCISSORS

Body Scissors have formerly been held in dread by most people as being excessively painful and difficult to break. However, the tactic described will enable the reader to escape from almost any scissors hold, whether from the front or rear.

POSITION: Your opponent has you with a front Body Scissors. You are face to face.

ACTION: 1. With all the strength at your command, dig your elbow into the soft tissue on the inside of your adversary's thigh (Fig. 49 and Fig. 50). His pain will be intense and should cause an immediate release.

Fig. 49

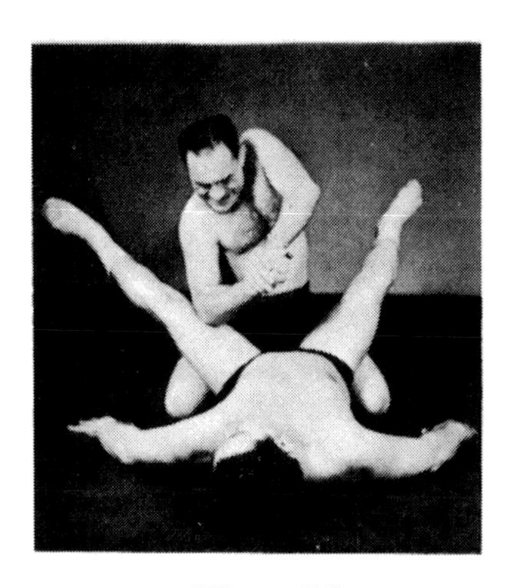

Fig. 50

BREAK FROM REAR BODY SCISSORS

The method described below will enable you not only to break this hold but also your enemy's leg or ankle. Because of this latter probability, be especially careful when practicing this hold on your partner.

POSITION: Your opponent has you with a rear Body Scissors (Fig. 51).

ACTION:
1. Cross your legs over his "scissors" (Fig. 52).
2. Throw your head back and your body forward. Your action will create terriffic pressure on his ankles. If you exert enough pressure, you will break his leg (Fig. 53).

Fig. 51

Fig. 52

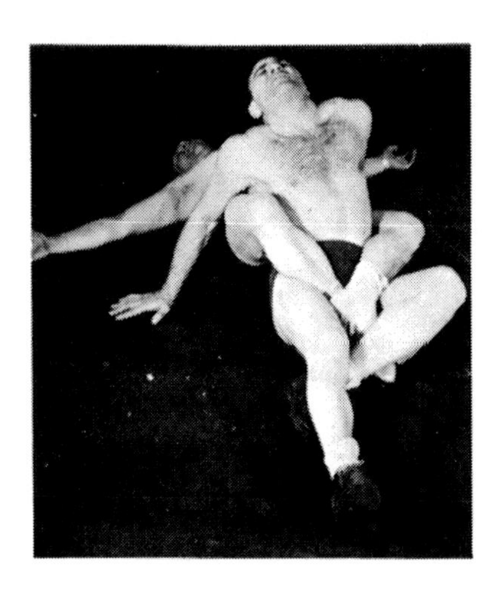

Fig. 53

BREAK FROM FULL NELSON

The Full Nelson is familiar to most men from boyhood days as an effective hold. However, the break from a Full Nelson can be mastered by following the procedure outlined below:

POSITION: Your opponent has applied a Full Nelson on you (Fig. 54).

ACTION:
1. Bend and twist your body to the left, bringing your left foot around opponent's leg.
2. Stand erect, lean backwards and drive your left elbow into his chest, or
3. Bend your body at the waist and grab opponent under his knees (Fig. 55). Then pick him off the ground as you stand erect. The last move is to fall backward, the entire weight of your body falling on him. This should succeed in breaking a few of his ribs (Fig. 56).

Fig. 54

Fig. 55

Fig. 56

BREAK FROM A HAMMER LOCK

The hammer lock is one of the most painful holds employed in combat and can be broken only with difficulty. However, it can be done by catching your opponent off guard.

POSITION: Your opponent has a hammer lock on you. (Fig. 57).

ACTION:

1. Bend your body forward at the waist. This movement will automatically straighten your captured arm (Fig. 58).
2. Then, stand erect and twist to the right (Fig. 59), if your right arm is held (or left if left arm his held), completing the action with a kick into your opponent's testicles (Fig. 60).

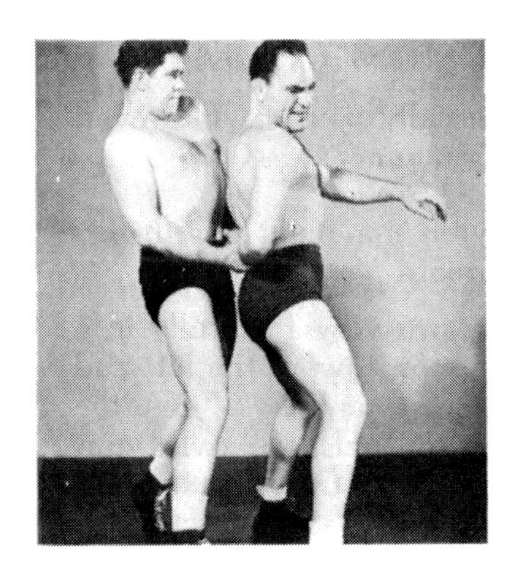

Fig. 57

Fig. 58

Fig. 59

Fig. 60

BREAK FROM FRONT FINGER STRANGLE

The front finger strangle is especially painful. However, it can be broken in the following manner:

POSITION: You are facing your opponent, his fingers grasping your throat.

ACTION:

1. Swing your right arm very forcefully in a long, overhead motion toward the left and over opponent's both arms (Fig. 61). At the same time bend at the waist and twist your body very vigorously at the waist toward your left (Fig. 62.) Your back is now turned to his back and both his arms are locked under your right armpit (Fig. 63). Hold on to his arms with your left hand, thus releasing your right arm. Then drive your right elbow backward with a crash into his face (Fig. 64). Or,
2. Hack both hands very vigorously at the soft tissue just above his hip bones. If you do this vigorously enough, as it should be done, he will collapse.

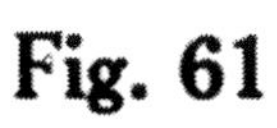

Fig. 61

Fig. 62

Fig. 63

Fig. 64

BREAK FROM GRAB BELT AND ELBOW

POSITION: Your opponent has your back arched over his bent leg, as shown in illustration (Fig. 65).

ACTION:

1. Wrap your right arm over and around the upper portion of his left arm. Retain this hold throughout this entire maneuver (Fig. 66).
2. With a sudden and sharp jerk twist your body to the left so that you are off his knee (Fig. 67). You will find that you have pulled your enemy off his feet and that his body is wrapped around your body (Fig. 68). He will be on his back. Now you can swing your fist into his groin.

Fig. 65

Fig. 66

Fig. 67

Fig. 68

BREAK FROM REAR STRANGLE

The Rear Strangle illustrated here is the traditional hold described in all Judo books as being unbreakable. However, it can be broken if you act before your opponent has the opportunity to bend your body backward.

POSITION: Your opponent has a Rear Arm Strangle on you (Fig. 69).

ACTION:

1. Reach up with either of your hands and clasp the hand he has about your head (Fig. 70).
2. Slide his arm upward and forward over your head. This arm will now be straight over your shoulder, the palm up (Fig. 71).
3. Now, with the aid of your other hand, bear down on his arm. If you exert sufficient pressure, you will break the arm at the elbow (Fig. 72).

Fig. 69

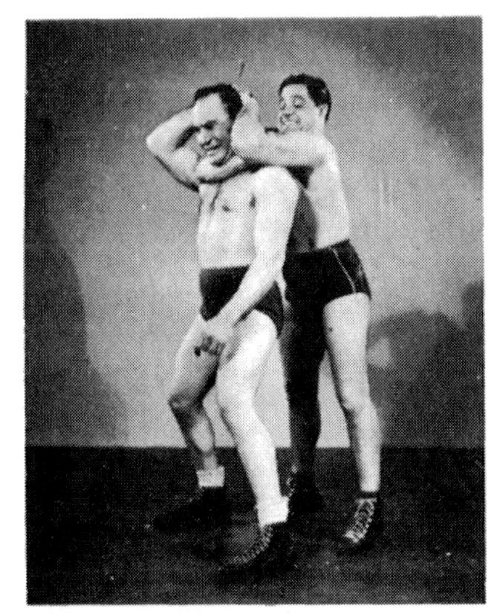

Fig. 70

Fig. 71

Fig. 72

BREAK FROM ARM STRANGLE

The arm strangle can easily be broken, particularly if your opponent is not given an opportunity to bend your body backward.

POSITION: Opponent has rear arm strangle on you.

ACTION:

1. Immediately turn your head away from his wrist which is pressing against your throat and turn your head toward the angle of his bent elbow. In this little space provided by the bend of his elbow you will find sufficient room to ease the pressure on your throat and thereby to catch a few gasping breaths while you prepare for your next move (Fig. 73).
2. Reaching up with your hands catch hold of the forearm around your neck and hang on to it tightly. Suddenly bend backward into his abdomen, pulling him forward and clear over your head. He will automatically let go to catch himself (Fig. 74).

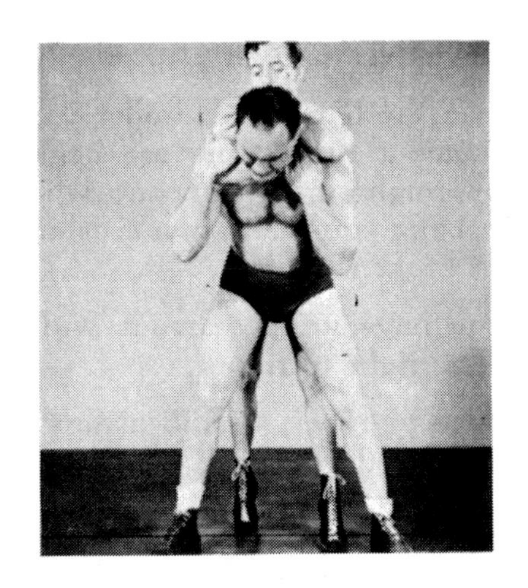

Fig. 73

Fig. 74

BREAK FROM HAND CLASP

You will encounter the hand clasp under various circumstances. Some combat maneuvers are begun from this position. Or you might meet someone who will try to impress you by seizing your hand in a crushing grip. This is how the hold is broken:

POSITION: You have gripped hands with your opponent, right to right.

ACTION: 1. Place your left thumb against the back of his right thumb (Fig. 75), faced in the same direction, and bend it back as far as possible (Fig. 76) This will immediately loosen his grip and you can slide your hand free.

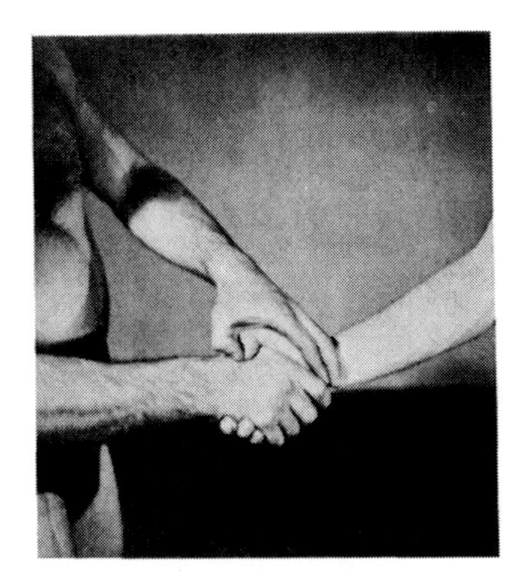

Fig. 75

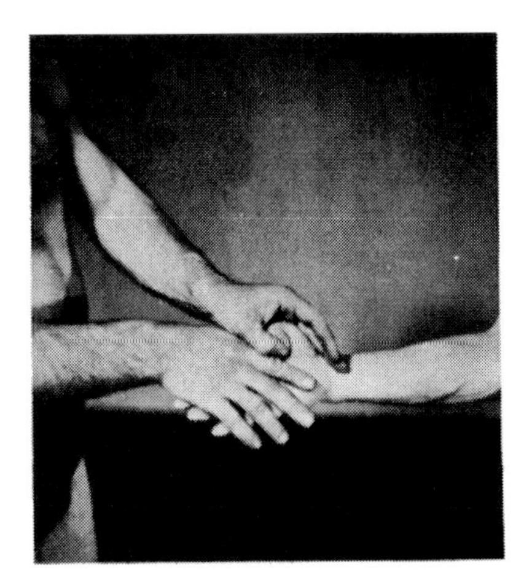

Fig. 76

BREAK FROM FRONT BEAR HUG

The Front Bear Hug is one of the most common and primitive of all holds. The escape is based on a series of short, simple moves, depending upon the nature of the hold.

POSITION: Your opponent has seized you in a front bear hug.

ACTION:
1. If your arms are encircled, bounce your head against your enemy's face, particularly his eyes, nose and teeth. At the same time, force your knee into his testicles.
2. In the event the bear hug has left your arms free,
   a) Circle your arm around his waist, jab your thumb beneath his ear, and force opponent to one side or the other in order to break his grip. Or,
   b) Force his head back by pulling at his hair and then hack at his throat (Fig. 77). Also force your knee into his testicles (Fig. 78). Or,
   c) Prod your left thumb into the base of his throat, your right thumb into his nose and force him back (Fig. 79), until you can deliver your knee into his testicles (Fig. 80).

NOTE: In exercising the above holds protect your testicles by turning your body to the right or left.

Fig. 77

Fig. 78

Fig. 79

Fig. 80

THROWS AND TRIPS

SHOULDER TWIST INTO STRANGLE

This is another maneuver which can be employed when you anticipate that your opponent is going to take the initiative.

POSITION: You are facing your opponent.

ACTION:
1. Place a hand on each of his shoulders and grasp a handful of clothes, or grasp his coat lapels, one in each hand (Fig. 81).
2. Vigorously twist his body around to one side by pushing one shoulder and pulling the other. This will spin him around sideways, placing your pushing arm in ideal position for strangling (Fig. 82).
3. Bend him backward; kick his near knee with your far foot (Fig. 83).

NOTE: You can achieve your objective more quickly by stepping around to his rear as you twist him.

Fig. 81

Fig. 82

Fig. 83

HIP THROW

The hip throw is a favorite Japanese trick used in close physical combat. A minimum of strength is required in its execution. It is primarily a matter of speed, leverage and balance.

POSITION: You are facing your opponent.

ACTION:
1. Place your left arm all the way around his waist leaving his right arm free (Fig. 84).
2. Pivot to the right on the right foot so that you are now both facing the same direction, with your back to his chest. At this point you may grasp his left wrist in your right hand if you can (although this is not necessary for the success of the operation). Then be sure that your left foot is far on the outside of his left foot so that your left hip extends a little past the left of his body (Fig. 85). In practice you should exaggerate this position a little more.
3. Bend forward to the right throwing your opponent over your left hip (Fig. 86).
4. As your opponent is being thrown, twist him around by pulling his left wrist towards the right and bringing your left knee under him so that when he falls he will lie prostrate and helpless across your knee (Fig. 87).

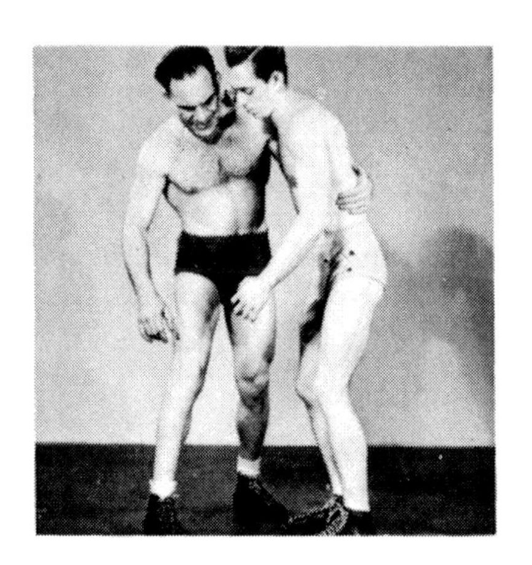

Fig. 84

Fig. 85

Fig. 86

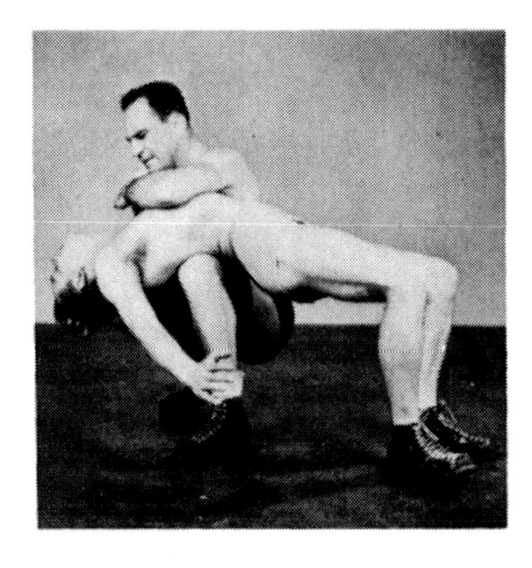

Fig. 87

SHOULDER THROW

The Shoulder Throw is very effective and spectacular. Moreover, it demands extraordinary speed to bring it to a successful conclusion. Once this throw is started, it is of the utmost importance that it be continued. Failure to execute the complete hold may result in your opponent's disabling you.

POSITION: You are facing your opponent.

ACTION:

1. Grasp opponent's right wrist in your left hand (Fig. 88). (This grip never changes throughout the entire procedure.) Raise your arm upward and to your left.
2. Pivot on your left foot with your back snug against your opponent's chest. You now both face in the same direction, and your right foot is outside his right foot. Keep his arm stretched over your shoulder. See Note below.
3. As you pivot, bring his right arm down over your right shoulder. With your right hand obtain a firm hold on his upper right arm. Your right hand must not slide down toward the elbow; the higher the grip of your right arm the more throwing leverage you have (Fig. 89).
4. Swing his right arm down in front of you in a sweeping motion. Dip your knees and at the same time thrust your hips back into his abdomen. This is important since it places you at a lower level than your opponent and makes the throw possible with a minimum of effort. At the same time twist to right and send him flying over your

Fig. 88

Fig. 89

Fig. 90

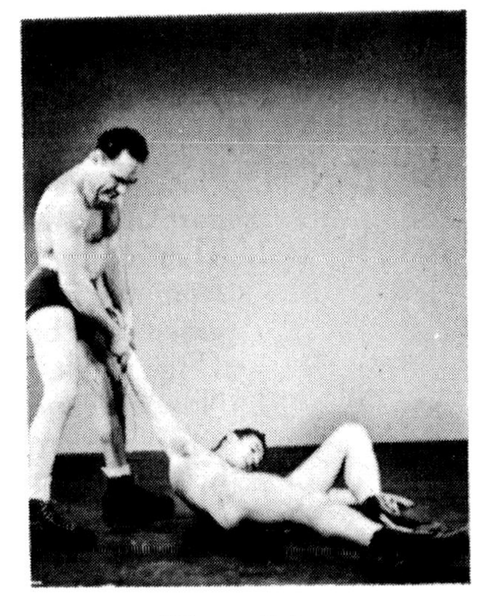

Fig. 91

SHOULDER THROW—(Continued)

shoulder to the ground. (Fig. 90). Now you either loose your grip on him so that he takes a hard fall or you hold on to his wrist (Fig. 91) and proceed as follows: As his body hits the ground, drop to your right knee and stretch his right arm, palm upward, across your left thigh. (Fig. 91). Pressure will break the arm.

NOTE: At this point, if you turn the palm of his captured arm up and bear down on the wrist, you can either break his arm at the elbow or go into a come along.

TIP OVER

This is one of the simplest methods of dropping an opponent when you are behind him.

POSITION: You are behind your opponent.

ACTION:
1. Place your left arm around his waist or any part of his upper body.
2. Then extend your hand through his crotch from the rear far enough so that you can grasp his belt, or a handful of clothing (Fig. 92).
3. Now lift and pull backward with the arm under the crotch so that he falls forward on his face (Fig. 93).

NOTE: This tip over is an excellent means of forcing an unwilling person through a door.

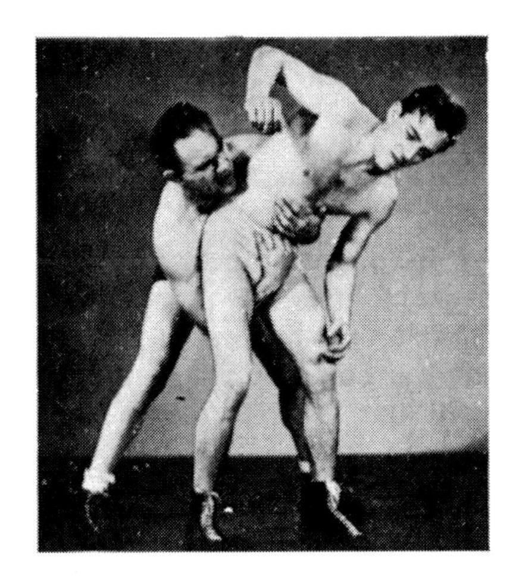

Fig. 92

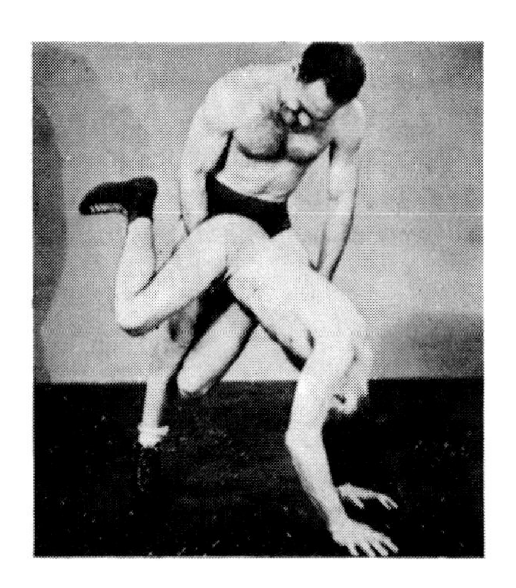

Fig. 93

COUNTER FOR CHEST PUSH

The following steps may be taken when pushed or grabbed in the region of the chest:

POSITION: You are facing your opponent.

ACTION:

1. As opponent attempts to grasp your clothes at your chest or places his hand on your chest to push you (Fig. 94), pin his hand to your chest by clapping the palms of both your hands tightly over the back of hand grasping above the bend of the wrist so that he cannot jerk it away (Fig. 95).
2. Then quickly bend your body forward from the waist (Fig. 96), dip your knees and twist your body away from opponent's free arm. He will then be forced to his knees to avoid fracturing his wrist (Fig. 97).

NOTE: To escape this hold, do not attempt to free hand by drawing it straight back. On the contrary bend it in the opposite direction of your opponent, and at the same time move your captured hand sharply down along the front of his body.

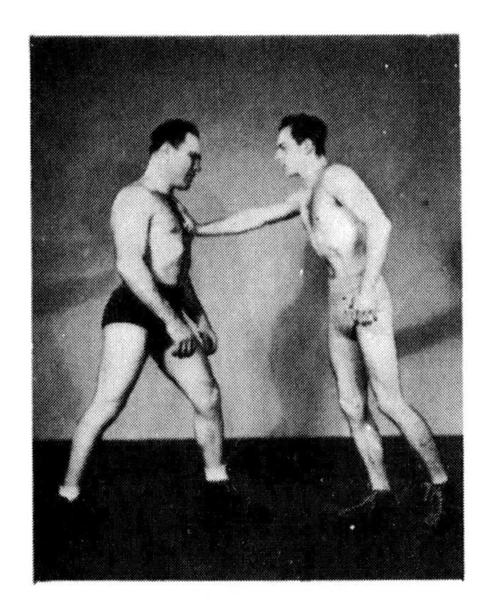

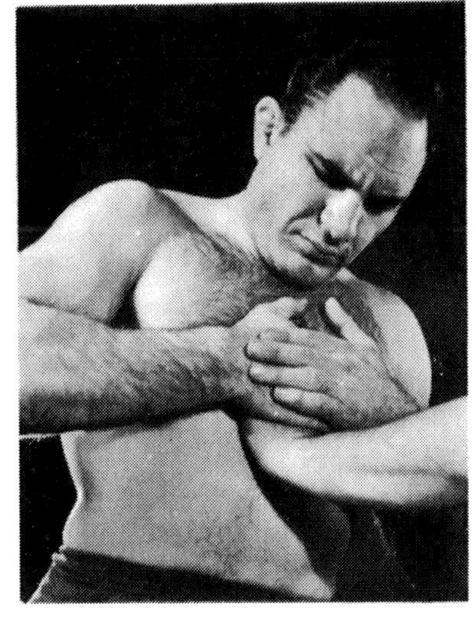

Fig. 94

Fig. 95

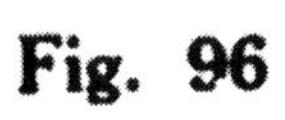

Fig. 96

Fig. 97

PILE DRIVER

This maneuver should be executed cautiously in practice as it can result in fracturing your opponent's neck.

POSITION: You are behind your opponent.

ACTION:
1. Encircle his waist with your left arm. Reach down with your right arm and grip his right knee (Fig. 98). Then pick him up bodily by means of the hold just secured (Fig. 99).
2. As you lift him you can easily turn him upside down so that his head is crashed to the ground. (Fig. 100 and Fig. 101.) See note.

NOTE: This process is simplified by lifting faster on the leg than on the waist. You may find it easier to lift your opponent by the following method: With your left arm around his waist, place your right arm through his crotch and clasp your left wrist, thus forming a saddle for your opponent to ride on the way up. Then merely stand up and tilt him over to the left and proceed as above.

Fig. 98

Fig. 99

Fig. 100

Fig. 101

ANKLE OR TROUSER CUFF JERK

The ankles or trouser cuffs can be used to throw your opponent.

POSITION: You are behind your adversary.

ACTION:
1. Drop to your knees and slide your hand down along his legs to his ankles. Grasp a trouser cuff in each hand, or, if you prefer, retain your hold on his ankles (Fig. 102).
2. Jerk the cuffs or ankles towards you, thus forcing your adversary to fall forward (Fig. 103).
3. A toe hold may now be applied (Fig. 104 and Fig. 105).

Fig. 102

Fig. 103

Fig. 104

Fig. 105

LAPEL THROW

If your opponent is wearing a coat with lapels, the following procedure will put him on his back very quickly.

POSITION: You are facing your opponent.

ACTION:
1. Grasp his right lapel securely in your right hand (Fig. 106)
2. Then twist your body to the left (Fig. 107) so that your back is to him (Fig. 108), and drop to your right knee. This action will pull him over your shoulder (Fig. 109).

Fig. 106

Fig. 107

Fig. 108

Fig. 109

TRIP FROM REAR

This action can easily be executed and is very effective. It is a simple variation of some of the more complicated rear trips.

POSITION: You are to the rear of your opponent.

ACTION:
1. Clasp both your hands around his waist and drop to your right knee (Fig. 110 and Fig. 111).
2. As you fall, twist your body to the left so that you are facing in that direction and extend your left foot straight ahead of you so that it is on the outside of your opponent's right foot (Fig. 112).
3. Continue this movement, kicking your opponent's right foot from under him with your left foot and pulling him down and to the right.
4. Your opponent is now on the floor. With your right hand you can proceed to hack at his neck or any other vulnerable area of his head or face (Fig. 113).

Fig. 110

Fig. 111

Fig. 112

Fig. 113

TRIP FROM BEHIND

There are innumerable methods of bringing an opponent down from the rear. The one described below can be executed by anyone.

POSITION: You are behind your opponent, your arms clasped around his waist (Fig. 114).

ACTION:
1. Twist slightly to the left and place your right foot back of his left knee (Fig. 115).
2. Force his left knee forward with your right foot as you twist him to the left and backward (Fig. 116).
3. Drop to your left knee to complete the fall.

Fig. 114

Fig. 115

Fig. 116

POLICE TACTICS

FIGHTING TWO MEN AT ONCE

This is a situation that may occasionally arise and is at best none too favorable, even for the Judo expert. Your only hope for victory lies in surprising your opponent and acting quickly.

POSITION: You are facing two opponents.

ACTION:

1. Your primary move is to center all your attention on one of the men by directing your conversation and gestures to him, thus temporarily allaying the suspicions of your second opponent.
2. Feint a hack at his throat (Fig. 117), then suddenly pivot toward the unprepared man, using the original force to carry the same blow to the latter (Fig. 118).
3. After this blow has landed, immediately pivot and kick to the testicles of the first man. This entire maneuver should not take more than three seconds (Fig. 119).

Fig. 117

Fig. 118

Fig. 119

ROPE STRANGLE

This is primarily a commando tactic. The primary objective is to steal up unobserved on a sentry. The rope strangle will be the only phase stressed here.

POSITION: You are stealing up on a sentry from the rear.

ACTION:
1. Cast rope (about two and one-half feet long) about sentry's neck (Fig. 120).
2. Immediately pull the rope back, against his throat and cross the ends of the rope by crossing your wrists as you turn your back to him (Fig. 121).
3. Draw the crossed ends of the rope over your shoulder as you bend forward (Fig. 122), thus raising his feet off the ground. The weight of his body against the taut rope will cause him to strangle (Fig. 123).

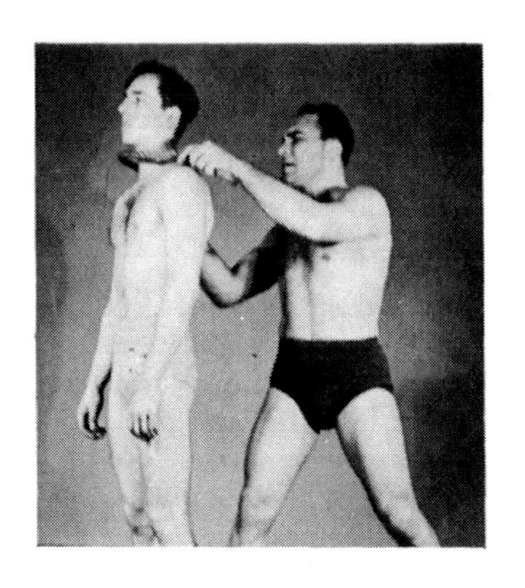

Fig. 120

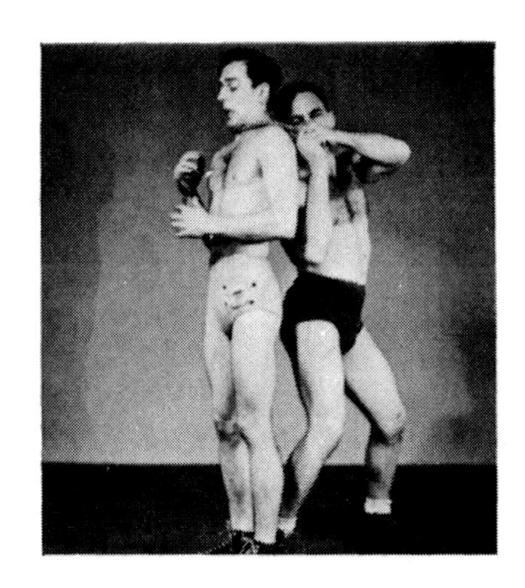

Fig. 121

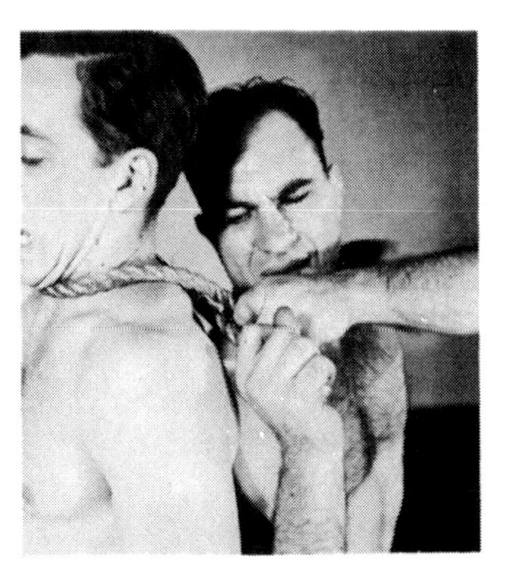

Fig. 122

Fig. 123

HAMMERLOCK COME-ALONG

This hold requires practice in order to achieve the speed and rhythmic action necessary for its successful performance.

POSITION: You are facing your opponent.

ACTION:
1. Grasp opponent's left wrist in your left hand (Fig. 124) and place your right hand on the upper portion of the captured arm. Now push up with your left arm and press down with your right one bending your opponent's arm (Fig. 125).
2. Throw this captured arm behind the upper portion of your right arm, bearing down with your right hand and pressing up with your elbow at the same time (Fig. 126).
3. Your right hand will now be free and you can utilize it to grasp your adversary's hair (Fig. 127).

Fig. 124

Fig. 125

Fig. 126

Fig. 127

REMOVING AN UNWILLING PERSON FROM A CHAIR

The following method is used to remove a stubbornly resisting person from a chair. Proceed as follows:

POSITION: Stand behind the seated person, facing the same direction in which he is facing.

ACTION:
1. Place your left arm or hand around his head (Fig. 128).
2. Then dig your right thumb into the soft tissue of his throat, at the angle of the jaw (Fig. 129). Press in and upward (Fig. 130). Your opponent's efforts will cease.

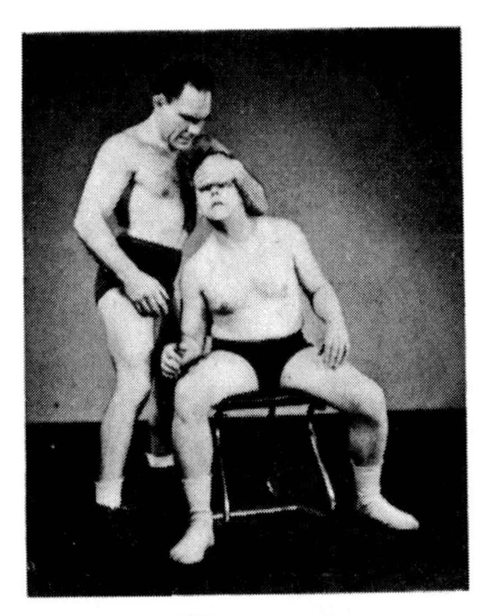

Fig. 128

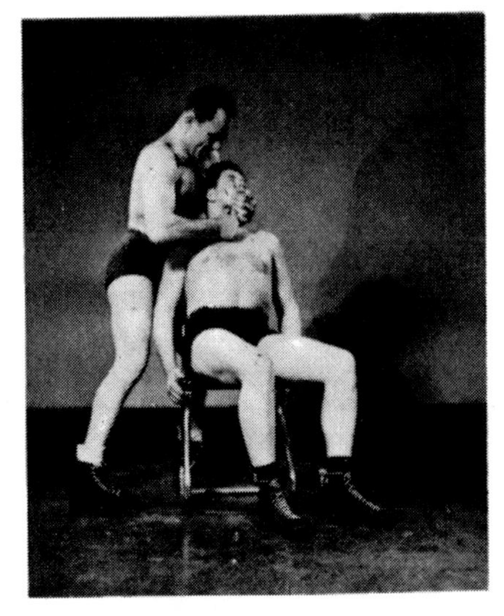

Fig. 129

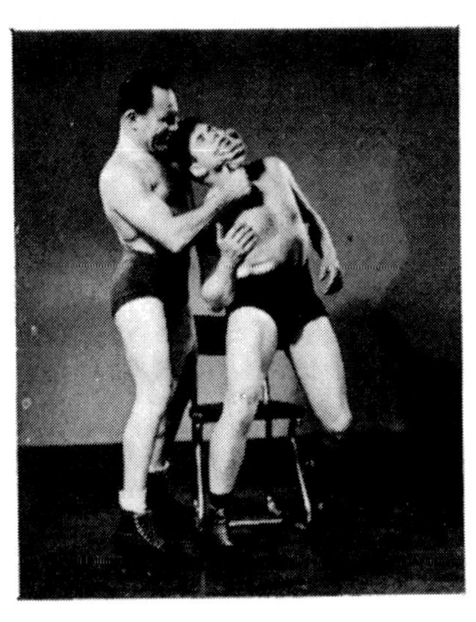

Fig. 130

DISARMING AN ASSAILANT WHO HAS A PISTOL POINTED AT YOUR BACK

POSITION: Your opponent has his gun pointed at your back (Fig. 131).

ACTION:
1. Keep talking to the enemy, saying anything that comes into your mind. Plead with him, break down and cry if you can, all in an effort to distract him from your planned action.
2. Keep the pistol against your back so that you are informed of its exact position. Furthermore, this will also prevent your opponent from constantly changing his position.
3. While you are talking to him learn in which hand your enemy is holding the pistol. You might do so by knowing his position, or by glancing out of the corner of your eye. At all times avoid revealing any intentions of your movements—such as changes in expression, or moving of your shoulder or any other such action.
4. If you have learned that the pistol is in your enemy's right hand, then suddenly and quickly twist your body to the right, your right elbow extended. Jab his pistol arm with your elbow and knock it out of the line of fire (Fig. 132).
5. Whether the gun goes off or not, continue the movement of your right arm and swing it up, under and around your opponent's pistol arm (Fig. 133).

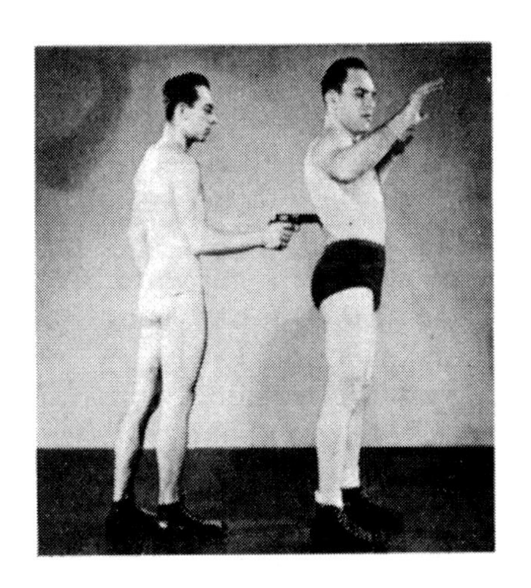

Fig. 131

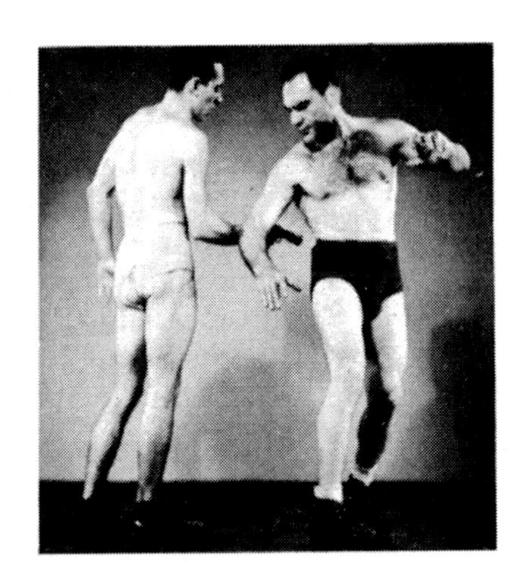

Fig. 132

Fig. 133

Fig. 134

DISARMING AN ASSAILANT WHO HAS A PISTOL POINTED AT YOUR BACK (Cont.)

6. Then bend forward, to the left, thus securing the arm holding the pistol between your arm and chest (Fig. 134).
7. Rapidly extend your left arm upward, grasping the pistol and tear it out of your opponent's hand (Figs. 135 and 136).
8. With the pistol in your possession, your opponent will expect the worst and will consequently be dangerous. Therefore, without any hesitation, slug your enemy against the side of the head with the gun (Fig. 137). Then place the gun in your shooting hand and be ready for anything (Fig. 138).

Fig. 135

Fig. 136

Fig. 137

Fig. 138

DISARMING AN ASSAILANT WHO IS FACING YOU WITH A PISTOL

To attempt to disarm your opponent of a dangerous weapon requires courage and good judgment. The attempt should be made only under circumstances of life and death.

POSITION: You are facing an opponent armed with a pistol.

ACTION: 1. The normal reaction when confronted by two objects raised at the same time is to concentrate on the higher object. Consequently, attempt this trick. When ordered to raise your arms raise the hand on the side of the pistol slower than the other (Fig. 139). The action must not appear deliberate nor hesitant. As your slow hand reaches the level of the pistol, drop it on the gun barrel and twist to the left; sway your body in the same direction to remove yourself from a direct line of fire (Fig. 140). See note.

2. If you are holding the gun barrel in your left hand, pivot to the left, your back to opponent. Then wrap your right arm around and under opponent's pistol arm, grasping your left wrist with your right hand (Fig. 141). Force the pistol backward and out of his hand, avoiding the line of fire (Fig. 142).

NOTE: If for some reason your hands are raised when confronted by your opponent, the action should be reversed. That is, drop your hands, the one closer to the gun going faster and, in the process, grasp the gun barrel and continue as set forth above.

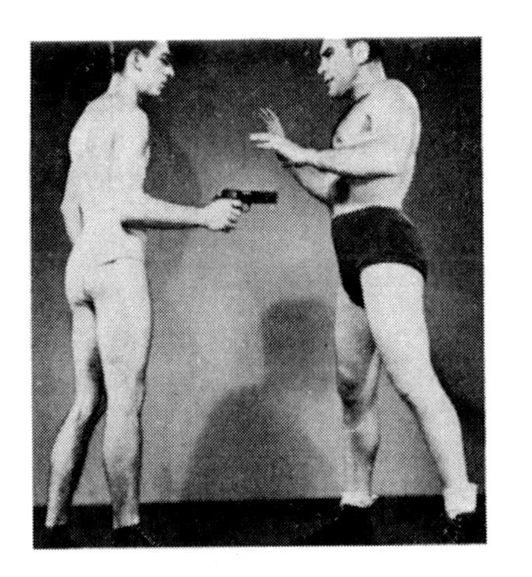

Fig. 139

Fig. 140

Fig. 141

Fig. 142

DISARMING AN OPPONENT OF A CLUB

The advantage you have in this situation is that a club is ordinarily less lethal and generally more unwieldy than a gun or a knife. The action described below is called the "Wrap Around."

POSITION: Your opponent intends to club you.

ACTION:
1. Block the blow by extending your left forearm against opponent's right (Fig. 143).
2. Slide your left arm around opponent's right elbow (Fig. 144).
3. Place your right hand upon his striking shoulder, at the same time grasping your right wrist with your left hand (Fig. 145).
4. Exert pressure with your left arm, pressing painfully up into the opponent's elbow.
5. Now you can either trip him to the ground by extending your right foot behind his right, or you can deliver your right knee into his testicles (Fig. 146). Throughout this action do not release his striking arm.

Fig. 143

Fig. 144

Fig. 145

Fig. 146

CROSSED ARM COME-ALONG

This is a very dangerous hold. Care should be exercised to protect your practice partner. Once you achieve the hold you are complete master of the situation.

POSITION: You are facing your opponent.

ACTION:
1. Grasp his right wrist in your left hand and his left wrist in your right hand (Fig. 147).
2. Cross your right arm under your left arm and twist to the left, bringing his crossed arms over your right shoulder. Your back will now be to his chest (Fig. 148).
3. If you intend no harm, merely bear down on his right wrist. This will cause pain and your opponent will be rendered helpless. If you are dealing with an enemy, apply pressure sharply downward and break his arm at the elbow (Fig. 149).

Fig. 147

Fig. 148

Fig. 149

RESUSCITATION

In the author's experience, the most effective method of reviving an unconscious victim is the one employed by the Japanese, called Kuatsu.

POSITION: The victim is lying unconscious on his back.

ACTION:
1. Stand at the side of victim's head and pick him up at his armpits into a sitting position (Fig. 150), raising him with a quick jerk. As you do so drive your knee sharply into his spine (Fig. 151) Deliver a blow with your fist to the same region, keeping the middle finger of your hand extended, but bent, to intensify the pain (Fig. 152).
2. Should the above fail to restore the victim to consciousness, pick him up and drive your knee into the base of his spine (Fig. 153).

Fig. 150

Fig. 151

Fig. 152

Fig. 153

TAKING AN UNWILLING PRISONER THROUGH A DOORWAY

At times you may find it necessary to remove an unwilling and stubborn person from one room to another, or to the street. This method will help you.

POSITION: Person refuses to be moved and has braced himself with his hands at the doorway.

ACTION:
1. Stand to the right and rear of the person.
2. Extend your right hand around his face so that your palm sets on the left side of his jaw. Place your left hand on the right side of his head (Fig. 154).
3. Now pull your right hand and push simultaneously with your left. You will twist his head so sharply to the right that his body will follow suit. Push him through the door (Fig. 155).
4. Another method is to grab his hair with your left hand, pulling his head back and at the same time punching his right buttock. This will force the person through the door (Figs. 156 and 157).

Fig. 154

Fig. 155

Fig. 156

Fig. 157

HOW TO SEARCH A PRISONER

Situation: You are an officer, and have stopped a suspicious looking person to search him. You are armed, but you must search him alone in such a manner that he cannot turn on you or disarm you.

POSITION: You are about to search a suspicious person.

ACTION:

1. Remain at least six feet away from the person. Hold your pistol at your right hip and do not extend your shooting arm because it might be captured and the pistol knocked out of your hand (Fig. 158).
2. Direct the person to face a wall or some other stationary object and to place his open hands thereon (Fig. 159).
3. Order him to cross his hands and his feet.
4. Now approach your prisoner and place your foot in front of his crossed feet. You can now proceed with the search (Fig. 160).

NOTE: At the slightest sign of a threatening move on the part of your prisoner, kick his crossed legs out from under him and he will fall on his face. Immediately step away from him so that he cannot secure a hold on your legs (Fig. 161).

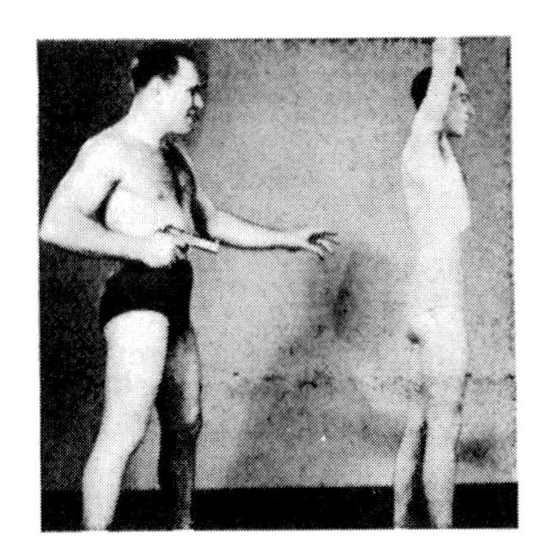

Fig. 158

Fig. 159

Fig. 160

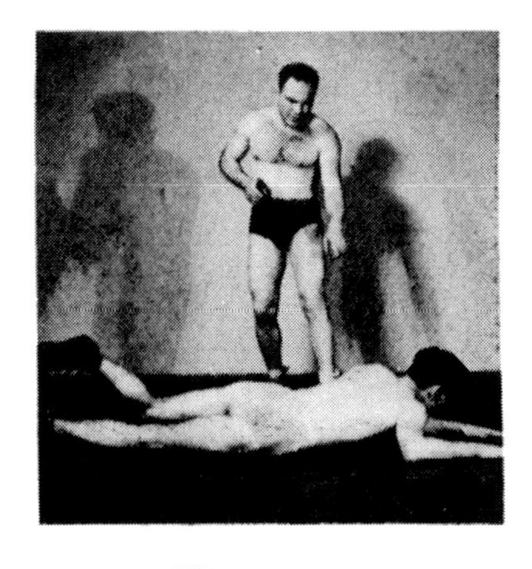

Fig. 161

BLOCKING HIP OR SHOULDER THROW

The Hip or Shoulder Throw is simple to block. No complicated counter hold is necessary.

POSITION: Your opponent has you in proper position and is about to apply the Hip or Shoulder Throw (Fig. 162).

ACTION: 1. As your opponent commences the throw, relax your body so that its entire weight counters his action and at the same time securely grab his pants with your free hand (Fig. 163). Or

2. Bring the knee opposite your captured arm sharply up into his buttocks, thus throwing him forward and off balance (Fig. 164). Or

3. Jab your free thumb into the soft tissue above his hip.

Fig. 162

Fig. 163

Fig. 164

DISARMING AN OPPONENT OF A KNIFE

It is difficult to disarm an opponent of a knife despite a common belief to the contrary. A knife is a light and dangerous weapon which can be wielded rapidly and in successive strokes. Consequently, the essence of this action is to avoid close contact with the enemy. The action described below has been tested and proven successful under various circumstances.

POSITION: You are facing an opponent armed with a knife (Fig. 165).

ACTION:
1. Twist your body to the left or to the right, bending in the same direction. Shift your body weight to one leg, the other bent as high as possible, ready to deliver a kick (Fig. 166).
2. Drive your bent leg into opponent's knee with all the force you can command (Fig. 167). This should succeed in breaking your enemy's leg. The least this action will do is to knock your opponent to the ground, thus granting you an opportunity to proceed to other holds described in this book.

Fig. 165

Fig. 166

Fig. 167

BLOCKING A KICK TO THE TESTICLES

You must be constantly on guard against a kick to the testicles. If it is attempted against you, block it in the following way so that you obtain a hold on your opponent's extended leg.

POSITION: You are facing an opponent who is directing a kick to your groin (Fig. 168).

ACTION:
1. Assume the defense position as in Fig. 169. Your body is bent forward slightly at the waist, one foot extended for balance. Your forearms are crossed in the shape of an "x."
2. Receive the kicking foot in the angle formed by your crossed arms. Close your arms around his ankle. The secret of this action is to permit his extended leg to come to you and not to reach down for it. If his kick is aimed at any of your vital organs it will reach into your extended arm (Fig. 170).
3. You now have your opponent standing off balance on one leg and can deliver to him the kick originally intended for yourself (Fig. 171).

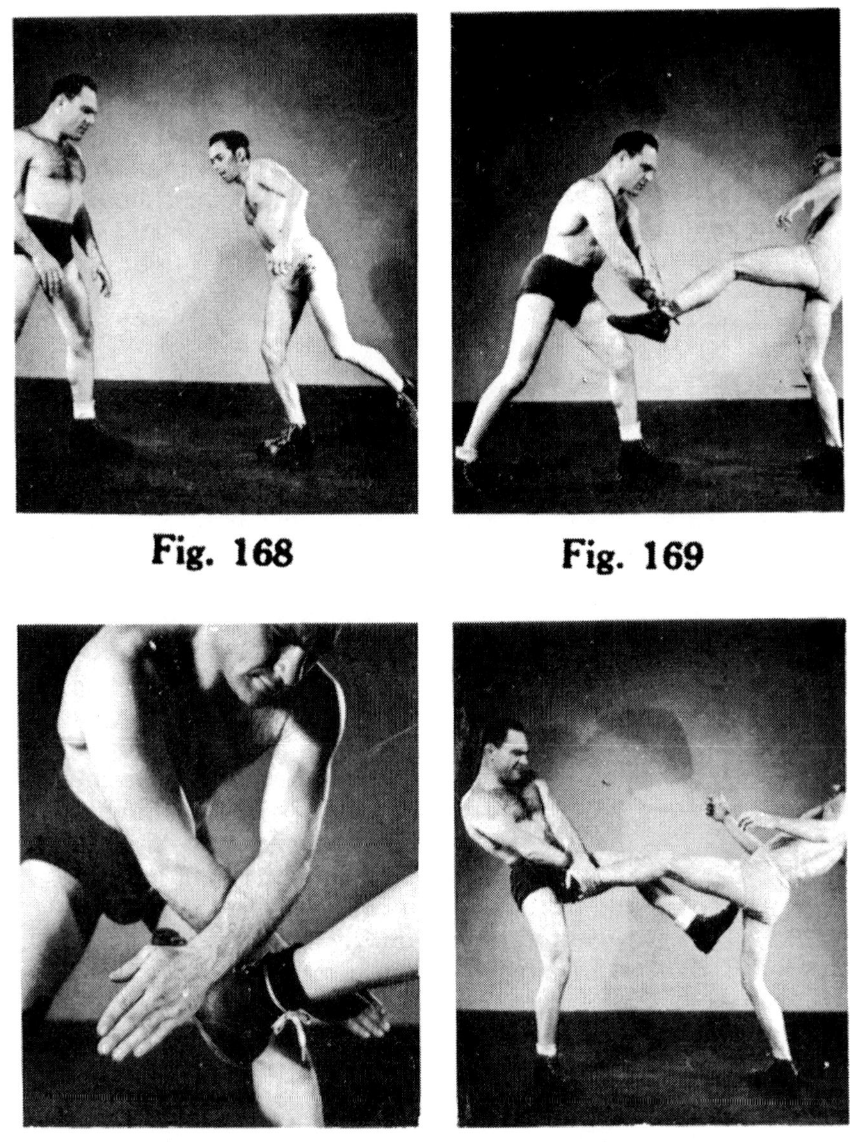

Fig. 168

Fig. 169

Fig. 170

Fig. 171

ARM HACK COME-ALONG

This hold is effective because of its simplicity of execution and the intense pain it produces. Come alongs are primarily used in police work on unruly persons. Drunks are somewhat impervious to such holds because alcohol produces an insensitivity to pain. The intoxicated person can be managed by a blow to his solar plexus which produces nausea and vomiting and will take all the fight out of him.

POSITION: You are facing your opponent.

ACTION:

1. With your right hand grasp opponent's right wrist and jerk his arm toward you (Fig. 172).
2. Simultaneously, pivot to the right and face in the same direction, keeping his arm stretched tightly across your chest (Fig. 173).
3. Throw your left arm over his right arm. If your opponent is particularly obstreperous, jab your left elbow into his face. (Fig. 174). If not, proceed to the next move.
4. Wrap your left arm over, under and around his right arm, just above his elbow. Secure your left arm by grasping your clothing at the chest, keeping your arm as high as possible. Your left arm is pressing into his right elbow. You can increase his pain by pressing down on his right wrist (Fig. 175). If your opponent refuses to come along you can break his arm.

Fig. 172

Fig. 173

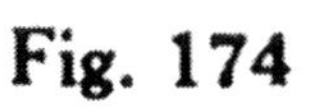

Fig. 174

Fig. 175

ARM TWIST

This hold requires a great deal of practice to obtain the necessary coordination and timing. However, once acquired, execution is simple.

POSITION: You are facing your opponent.

ACTION:
1. Grasp opponent's right wrist in your right hand. Cup your left hand and place it behind his right elbow (Figs. 176 and 177).
2. Raise and bend his captured arm as you make an about face. His arm is now bent over the right shoulder (Fig. 178).
3. Pull him back and wrap your left arm around his right elbow (Fig. 179).

Fig. 176

Fig. 177

Fig. 178

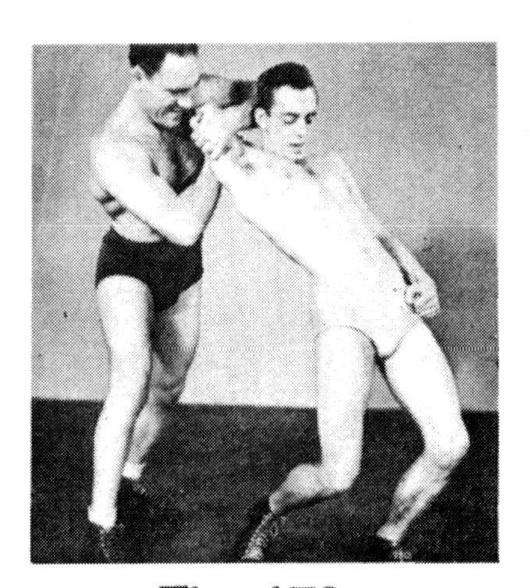

Fig. 179

WRIST LOCK COME-ALONG

This come-along when correctly applied, is very effective. A little practice will make its application smooth and flowing.

POSITION: You are facing your opponent.

ACTION:
1. Grab his right wrist with your right hand and jerk his arm to you.
2. As you apply the jerk, close in at his right and hook your left forearm under and around his right biceps as tightly as possible. Retain this pressure (Fig. 180).
3. Bend opponent's right arm slightly above your left hip, holding it in this position. This arm must not be permitted to slide, or rest on your chest or abdomen (Fig. 181).
4. Place your left hand on his wrist, behind your right, for additional support.
5. Without removing your right hand, slide it beneath his wrist, your thumb leading, to exert pressure on the under side of his wrist (Fig. 182).
6. Now apply opposing pressure with both your hands and bend his wrist double. This will cause him to extend his thumb.
7. With your left thumb stationary, gather in his thumb with your left fingers and draw it toward his wrist.
8. Finally, free your right hand and grasp his right small finger. Bend it back (Fig. 183). It requires little pressure to break. The pain will be terrific and your opponent can be led anywhere.

Fig. 180

Fig. 181

Fig. 182

Fig. 183

ATTACK FROM THE GROUND

In any conflict between two opponents, the ground work is very important. Many men are quite effective as long as they are on their feet, but seem to lose all combative ability when they are on the ground.

POSITION: You are on the ground in any position, facing your opponent (Fig. 184).

ACTION:
1. Take a rolling leap to your opponent's legs with the left side of your body leading.
2. As your left side contacts his forward leg, immediately wrap your left arm, from the outside, around his ankle (Fig. 185).
3. Continue the twisting roll of your body in the same direction, pulling his leg forward as you roll, thus forcing him to fall backward (Fig. 186).
4. Drive your right elbow into his testicles (Fig. 187).

Fig. 184

Fig. 185

Fig. 186

Fig. 187

SITUATIONS

RELEASE ATTACK AND DEFENSE ATTACK

I. Being Attacked from Rear
 A. Grasp testicles
 B. Elbows or fists in ribs
 C. Stamp on shin bones and instep
 D. Kick backwards at shins or testicles
 E. Bend over, pull foot through
 F. Tear fingers away
 G. Hip throw (if arms are over your shoulders)
 H. Pin arms with your elbows if he reaches under your arms
 I. Snake around behind with legs and throw him
 J. Double wristlock
 K. Raise arms with force and slide down through (if grabbed over your arms)
 L. Grapevine legs, if he picks you up
 M. Swing and go behind, if he picks you up

II. Being Strangled with Hands
 A. For front strangle, bring hands up forcibly and out through center; hack down on neck; kick with foot or knee

III. Being strangled with Forearm
 A. Releases
  1. Duck chin
  2. Turn head toward elbow
  3. Grab forearm and try to pull it away
 B. Tear fingers away; arm swing and pin arms, kick knee; apply wrist twist

IV. Being Grasped by the Wrists
 A. Kick or use knee
 B. Pressure against thumbs
 C. Cross-over break

V. Being Attacked While Lying Face Down
 A. Roll over on back
 B. Raise legs and kick

C. Pivot so that feet aim at opponent and kick
D. Kick opponent's knee, or hook his ankle
E. If opponent jumps at you, roll out of his way and onto your feet

VI. Being Rushed Head-On
A. Grasp arm or coat lapels and execute hip throw
B. Feint high, then fall at opponent's feet and trip him
C. Kick at testicles or knee-cap

VII. Fighting Face to Face
A. Attack
1. Kick or use knee
2. Grab belt and thrust forearm to throat
3. Go-behinds (arm drag)
4. Step behind, trip, and use "Iron claw" to face
5. Wrist-twist
6. Come-alongs
7. Hip throw
8. Front strangle or neck-breaker defense

B. Defense
1. The perfect stand
2. Ready to block knee or kick
3. Ready to parry boxing blows
4. Ready to parry knife attacks

C. Releases
1. Wrist twist
2. Arm breaker (down with armpit at elbow)
3. Kick or use knee
4. Wrist lock come-along
5. Hip throw
6. Hacking at arm or neck, etc.

VIII. Making an Attack From Rear
A. Pull head back, exert pressure at base of spine